Published by Sterry and Sterry, Inc.
www.anne-louise.com / www.auntlena.com

Project Management by Charlie Clark Books, llc / www.charlieclarkbooks.com
Design by Susan Bard / www.susanbarddesign.com
Editing by Indigo Edition and Publications / www.indigoediting.com
Photographs on cover and pages 2, 3, 4 by Kevin McInroy-Edwards.
Illustrations on pages 51, 52, 53 by Maggie Olson.

ISBN 13:9780615289175

Printed and bound in the United States by Color House Graphics, Inc.

Aunt Lena's Cucina

Mangi per Vivere,
Viva per Amare!

Eat to Live,
Live to Love!

Dedicated to my darling Mama,
La Principessa delle sfere di carne.
Viva la Famiglia!

"I'm saying yes ta Joy!"

Acknowlegements:

My Bobby, for his love, support and humor.

Charlie Clark, for his gentle prodding and critical help
in bringing Aunt Lena to a wider world.

Susan Bard, for the same reason with saintly patience.

Ali McCart, for making Aunt Lena readable, accessible and publishable.

Kevin McInroy-Edwards, for making Aunt Lena a fashion icon,
and encouragement to just go for it.

Italy, for the genes.

America, for the opportunity.

"Wadda yas wanna know?"

So wadda ya wanna know about me? I'm old —that's fa sure—which means I was born a long time ago! I came from the old country when I was a bambino. We settled around Hoboken, New Jersey, and the Bronx, New York. There were a lot of girls in my family. Wadda ya gonna do?!

I gotta lotta things to tell yas about my life when I come to visit. I'll bring some gravy, we'll have macaroni.

Oh … ya makin' your own gravy now from my recipe? Heh heh, good for youse. I'll still bring mine. We can tawlk about things.

By da way, I'm lookin' for a new husband … this time fa love! 'Cause I already had two husbands before, which I married fa money. In my family we had a saying … marry first time fa money, second time fa love. I had to marry two times fa money —da first one didn't have enough! Any of youse got a nice handsome relative ya like to introduce me to? If he's rich, that's OK too. Love and money go together like a horse an' carriage!

"I'm thinkin' of a recipe fa youse."

My Story and Recipes

"If chicken soup is Jewish penicillin, then pasta fagioli is Italian aspirin with an extra dose of love added! A leisurely stroll through the pages of this book will take you on a wonderful journey into a life that is an example of the best of cutting edge Mediterranean wisdom illustrated by some superb recipes."

Aunt Lena dreams of America.

From My Kitchen Table:

I'm sittin' here at my kitchen table, thinking about all youse who are reading my book. Wadda I gotta tell ya? So many things about cookin' and food and love come into my mind.

Ya know there's so many ways ta cook Italian 'cause Italy is a bigga place. Every family has their own way. But it's always about love!

Ya love ya family so ya cook fa dem. Ya love ya friends so ya cook fa dem. It makes ya feel good and makes them feel good too. Yas gotta laugh while ya cookin' too 'cause it's good fa ya soul. And tell all the old stories and sing all the old songs.

And did ya know that if ya laugh two hundred times it's like being on one a dem rowing machines fa ten minutes? I'm a telling yas this 'cause I am an up-ta-date lady, and I like ta share all these good things wid my friends. Joosta little aside!

When ya cook these recipes, let ya kids or ya grandchildren or any kids that are around, let them all help ya. There's nothing so nice as cookin' wid the little ones. It doesn't matter if it is not "perfect," 'cause this is not about perfect. It's about making traditions, and that's about love.

Ya know the kids rememba and they will wanna come and help ya at the next holiday or family time. And again and again and again.

Sometime when they are big and have moved away from ya (though why they move away, I do not know!!) they will rememba still and start their own traditions, cookin' wid their kids. And so it gets passed down along wid the stories ya tell while ya cookin' and the songs ya sing together. I'm tellin' ya, nothing can replace this. I know 'cause I am old.

And it all comes from making my recipes!!

On the plane from Rome, Aunt Lena enjoys one of the perks that come with being an international fashion icon. Free flowing wine!

"It doesn't matter if it is not 'perfect,' 'cause this is not about perfect. It's about making traditions, and that's about love."

Back ta cookin'. Used ta be in the old days when I was young, I thought only our way was good. Now I know that all ways ta cook are good, but I can only share wid yas my way 'cause that is all I know. I got lots of simple recipes fa everyone in this book, even if youse are joosta learning to cook.

Aunt Lena arrives in New York and soon gets the hang of the big city.

Ya know lots of the recipes are very healthy and don't cost so much money. 'Cause fa things to taste good, they don't have ta be fancy, they don't have ta make ya sick, and they don't have to rob ya pocketbook. This is something my family knew a lot about! I'll bet ya feel relieved now that I told yas that. Makes ya wanna joosta start cookin', don't it?

Some of these recipes I learned from my nonna and some from my mamma. My mamma learned from her nonna and even from her husband's family. Though my family comes from around Napoli, not all the recipes do. (I know ya like all these little facts.)

Now if yas have any problems, ya can call me or email me and I can help ya out. If ya need some stories ta tell, I got those too! I wanna be sure ya have all da help ya can get … 'cause I know some of youse need it! Do you know in some parts of this country people think there is ketchup in spaghetti gravy?! So I try ta educate people about the real thing! Doesn't mean the

ketchup dish is not good, but when youse taste my gravy … ahhh.
Well, you decide. It tastes different, that's fa sure.

When youse makes ya first recipe from da book, ya invite ya family and
friends over. Maybe it's Sunday even. Youse all sit down wid a nice glass of
wine — or no wine if ya don't drink wine … I mean no disrespect. 'Cause
if ya ain't got respect, wadda
ya got? Ya got nothin'. Yas
all smile at each other,
give thanks and mangiare
(that's "everybody eat" in
Italian). What could be
better than that? Everyone
saying how good this food
is, asking how did ya do
it, tawlking, laughing …
so much love flowing. It'sa
nice, no?

Dat's why ya gotta cook
yaself. Don't go and buy that
gravy from a jar and all that
frozen stuff. Youse can do it, I
promise!!

Whad else can I tell yas in
this short space? We need days
and days together — I got so much I could tell yas.

"I found a nice
place here."

Ooh fa … it's late. No more time
fa tawlking. I gotta go to church and light some candles. Time to put on my
hat and gloves. A lady don't go outside widout her hat an' gloves. And I gotta
put my lipstick on too, 'cause a lady don't go out widout her lipstick either.
(Did I get it on my teeth, dolls?)

Don' faget ta let me know when yas want me ta come visit and cook wid ya.
Joosta call me!

Ciao, bella!

Spaghetti Gravy

Or "sauce," for youse who thinks ya got fancy pants!

Makes about 4–6 cups *(enough fer a pound a'pasta)*

1 very large onion, finely chopped
2 cloves garlic, finely chopped
1 large handful of fresh parsley, chopped
Water, maybe ¼ cup
2–3 Tbsp. olive oil
1 lb. of minced beef if ya want meat sauce
1 small (6-oz.) can tomato paste
1 large (28-oz.) can of tomato puree

> (Now, in some places ya can't get puree. Wadda ya gonna do? Well, ya can use yer own tomatoes that ya grew in the summer and just make puree by putting 'em in da food processor. In the old days, we just chopped them up finely by hand, but now we got tings like food processors. If ya didn't grow them, ya can buy canned tomatoes and puree them. Don't buy tomato sauce 'cause it has too much salt and other bad tings. Ya gotta trust me on this. Back to da recipe …)

Oregano
Basil
Salt and pepper
1–2 cups stock—chicken or beef, whatever ya got on hand.
> Homemade is best, but if not then the kind in da cans or boxes. Ya know what I mean?

No sugar—yas don't need that!

Take the onion, garlic, and parsley, and put it in ya big gravy pot with a little water. Bring it to a boil and cook da water out while stirring. Make sure ya don't burn it, which is why ya gotta keep stirring and watching!

Then take ya bottle of olive oil, hold it over da pot, and pour in about 2–3 Tbsp.

"Here we are wid da gravy recipe. This is da first thing ya gotta learn fa ya cooking—that's why I put it first! 'Cause gravy is like ya life's blood, ya know wad I mean?

Gravy—ya gotta make yer own. It's like you—different and special, not like anyone else. If ya don't make yer own gravy, ain't nobody gonna do it fa you. Ya know, it's like happiness, ya gotta find it yerself—a hard fact of dis life, but so true!"

"Three times around da pot wid ya olive oil" is what my mamma used ta say. Stir again.

Here ya add ya beef if ya want, and brown it well. After da meat is browned, add the tomato paste and brown that while ya stir again.

Now add ya big can of puree, ya spices and ya stock. Start wid 1 cup of da stock, bring to a boil, then reduce heat and simmer, covered, fer about 2 hours.

More time if ya got it— da longer da better.

Ya don't want it ta be too soupy, so only add more stock if it seems too thick. If it gets too soupy, just take da cover off and keep cookin'. It will thicken up as it cooks.

Keep stirring every now an' again.

A few more tips:

It is even better the second day!

Ya can add any meat ya want instead of minced beef— even fish is good. In fact, anything in gravy is good! If ya don't eat meat, use vegetable stock and no meat. It is still so delicious.

From this gravy, ya can make so many other tings, so practice practice!

"Badda Bing, Badda Bang!"

"ya know, my great-niece Anne-Louise who tinks she's a star, well it took her a long time ta understand that makin' gravy and makin' yer own life are one and the same ting.

So I wrote dis little song ta help her along da way. Youse can sing it while ya makin' da gravy and well, sing it all da time to keep ya feeling so good. (Did youse know dat singing raises the feel-good hormones? Badda bing badda bang ... need I say more?)"

Gravy Song

Lyrics © Aunt Lena, aka Anne-Louise Sterry, September 2003

Sung to the tune of "Funniculì, Funniculà"

(Dis melody was written by Italian composer Luigi Denza in 1880).

Verse 1

When I was young I loved to be a victim.

It was so true, it was so true.

I said it's not my fault, it always is them.

They make me blue, they make me blue.

But now I am a grown up and I know this:

I have a choice, I have a choice.

To create my happiness is what I will do.

I found my voice, I found my voice.

CHORUS

Gravy, gravy, it will take ya far.

Gravy, gravy, don't get it from a jar.

You make your own, you make your own, you make your own,

Not from a jar.

Making your own gravy

Feels like flying on a star.

Verse 2

Sometimes I find it hard to always do this.

And so will you, and so will you.

To make a change, I know, is such a big risk.

For dreams to brew, for dreams to brew.

You'll walk a step ahead then a step backwards.

It makes you scream, it makes you scream.

Don't stop, don't change your mind, keep walking forward.

You'll catch your dream, you'll catch your dream.

CHORUS

Verse 3

Perhaps you find it hard. You don't believe me.

You think I'm wrong, you think I'm wrong.

You say I must be nuts, it's not so easy

To change your song, to change your song.

But me, I am a model for this lesson.

Though I am old, though I am old.

I know its not too late to find your passion.

You must be bold, you must be bold.

CHORUS

Meatballs

Ya gotta have 'em.

Makes about a dozen meatballs

4 handfuls fresh bread crumbs from day-old Italian bread
1 lb. minced beef
1 egg
1 large handful of mixed grated cheese (Romano and Parmesan)
½ handful fresh parsley
Salt and pepper
¼ tsp. garlic powder
2 Tbsp. oregano
Olive oil

"Hands off those meata balls!"

First ya let me tell yas about da bread crumbs: Ya can use a food processor, if ya got one, to make da crumbs. If not, then do like we did in the old days—just tear da bread up wid ya hands. After ya make them, put a little water on the crumbs, and squish this wid ya hands. Ya want the crumbs moist but not soaked.

Mix the bread crumbs along with the beef, egg, cheese, parsley, salt and pepper, garlic powder, and oregano together in a large bowl.

Then put a little olive oil on da palms of ya hands. Take some of da mixture and form it into balls, maybe about 2 inches in diameter.

But yas can make them whatever size ya want. Keep ya hands moistened wid da oil. (Olive oil is good fa ya skin too; makes ya hands nice and soft.)

Take a nice cast-iron fry pan if ya got it. If not, well wadda ya gonna do? Use da fry pan dat ya got!

Put in some olive oil, heat it up over medium heat, and fry da meatballs, turning 'em over and over ta get all sides done.

Now once they are done, ya can put 'em in the gravy or just pop them in ya mouth one by one until they are all gone, 'cause ya won't be able ta stop eating 'em!

"If ya think ya've had meatballs, wait till ya make these. Youse will never want the ones from da restaurants again! It's like da gravy ... ya gotta do it yerself."

"We gotta a lotta
minestrone on the stove
... come on over!"

Minestrone Soup

Serves 4–6

1 tsp. olive oil
⅛ lb. salt pork, diced
1 clove garlic, chopped
1 small onion, chopped
1 tsp. chopped parsley
1 tsp. chopped basil
3 tomatoes, chopped
3 stalks celery, chopped
2 carrots, sliced
2 white potatoes, peeled and sliced
1 small turnip, peeled and diced
Half small cabbage, shredded
2 zucchini, diced
1½ quarts water
Salt and pepper
1 (15-oz.) can red kidney beans, rinsed and drained
1 cup ditalini rigati or any other small pasta
Parmesan cheese

In a large pot or saucepan, heat da olive oil, add ya salt pork, garlic, onion, parsley, and basil. Brown lightly.

Add ya tomatoes, celery, carrots, potatoes, turnip, cabbage, zucchini, water, and salt and pepper.

Bring to a boil, then reduce heat and simmer for 45 minutes.

Add da beans and the ditalini. Cook 10 more minutes until the ditalini is tender.

Serve sprinkled with Parmesan cheese.

Note: Yas can add white beans, string beans, peas, corn—whatever vegetables are in season.

"Now this here soup is something ta make yer heart sing on a cold winter night! Bake some nice crusty bread, have a little wine, and wadda ya got? Ya got what yas really need ... love!"

"Now this here is good."

Steak Pizzaiola with Spaghetti

Serves 4–6

3 Tbsp. olive oil
2 Tbsp. water, more or less
1 lb. top sirloin or chuck steak
1 large (28-oz.) can chopped tomatoes with juice
Salt
1 Tbsp. parsley
2 cloves garlic
1 lb. spaghetti
Parmesan cheese

Put olive oil and water in a large skillet and heat togetha.

Add the meat, and brown on both sides.

Add the tomatoes, salt, parsley, and garlic. Simmer for 40–45 minutes.

Slice the meat and serve with cooked spaghetti, gravy (see page 8) and Parmesan cheese. Youse may also serve the meat separately with vegetables, saving the gravy for another meal with spaghetti.

So ya got two meals here for the price of one. Not so bad, heh heh!

"Ya know ya gotta have steak for da men. It makes them feel good and strong ... which is how ya want ya man ta feel when he takes ya in his arms. Need I say more? Badda bing, badda bang!"

Traditional Cheese-Filled Manicotti

"Tradition ... ya gotta have traditions in ya family. They help keep ya together, which is what it is all about, ya know what I mean? So ya make this manicotti like in da old days. None of this fancy manicotti wid lobster or gorgonzola or ham and pineapple. Da ol' kind keeps the ol' ones happy and makes tradition wid ya kids too. No matter what is going on in da world, da traditions ya family has keep everybody feeling loved. And dat's what it is all about!!"

Serves 4–6

Filling:

2 lbs. ricotta cheese

2 eggs

1 Tbsp. parsley, chopped

Salt and pepper

4 Tbsp. mixed, grated Romano and Parmesan cheese

Mix all ingredients together in bowl. Set aside.

Crepes:

2½ cups cold water

2½ cups flour

6 eggs

1 tsp. salt

Olive oil

Parmesan cheese

1 recipe Gravy (see page 8)

Mix water, flour, eggs, and salt together in a medium bowl. Beat well.

In a crepe pan, add just enough olive oil to coat the pan. Heat pan, making sure to get it hot without burning the oil. Pour in enough batter to make a thin crepe.

Cook on one side till nearly set, like yas do wid pancakes.

Flip crepe over and cook 3–5 seconds on the other side. Crepes should be light and thin.

Ya might have ta try one or two ta get it right!

Batter makes about 50 crepes.

18

Now preheat the oven ta 350°F.

Cover the bottom of a baking dish with gravy.

Stuff each crepe with 1 or 2 Tbsp.
of the filling. Roll up and
invert crepe in the baking dish.

Fill the dish with a single layer of crepes, and then
cover with more gravy.

Bake for 30 minutes or until nice and hot.

Serve sprinkled with Parmesan cheese.

This is so delicious and so easy
ta make. If ya have a problem
eatin' the ricotta, get da
skim milk kind and maybe take
da pills fa milk problems. 'Cause
ya don't wanna have troubles
with ya insides when ya got
family and friends
at ya house!

Aunt Lena Says...

Ya Gotta Make Your Own Gravy...!

Meat and Cheese Lasagna

Serves 8–10

youse can make lasagna with meat or without. It's better with da meat, though.

1 lb. Italian sausage
1 recipe Meatballs (see page 12)
9 oz. lasagna noodles or one box
2 recipes Gravy (see page 8)

Cook the Italian sausage. After cookin', cut the sausage in small pieces. Set aside. Cut the meatballs into small pieces and set aside. Youse can do all the above steps a day or two before, if yas like. Then it's not so much work on one day.

Cheese Filling:
2 lbs. ricotta
4 cups shredded or chopped mozzarella.
Get the fresh — it is much better!
1 egg
1 Tbsp. parsley
Salt and pepper
3 Tbsp. mixed grated cheeses (Romano and Parmesan)

Preheat the oven ta 350°F.

Mix all filling ingredients in a large bowl.

Now yas are ready to assemble ya lasagna. For this ya need a box of lasagna noodles.

Then … take a 9 x 12 baking dish, and cover the bottom with a generous amount of gravy.

"ya make this and ya friends are gonna tink they died and went ta heaven! Never have they had anything so good 'cause usually they buy da frozen lasagnas at those big stores. But this is the real thing. It is worth da time it takes ta make, fa sure. ya friends will know ya love them after they eat this. And besides, yer teaching them what good food is all about."

Now lay the *uncooked* lasagna noodles in the bottom of the dish to make one layer.

Cover that layer with the ricotta mixture, followed by chopped sausage and meatballs, then gravy.

Keep making da layers till ya have none of da ricotta mixture left.

Youse can sing a song or two while ya doing this ta make da time go by!

"Boy, dis is one lucky fella!"

End with a layer of noodles and a lot of gravy. Ya can sprinkle the top with shredded mozzarella and Parmesan if ya like. Now cover it tightly with aluminum foil and bake for 90 minutes. Ya can uncover it for the last 10 minutes to crisp up the top if youse like it like that.

Serve with more gravy and grated cheese.

This is a meal fit fer a king or queen! And a nice glass of red wine will help cut the cholesterol too!!

"Is it on my teeth, dolls?"

Chicken Cacciatore

Serves 4–6

1 chicken, cut up
1 large (28-oz.) can crushed tomatoes
1 or 2 onions, sliced
1–2 cups black olives, sliced
1 or 2 green peppers, sliced
1 Tbsp. olive oil
2 Tbsp. water
Oregano and basil (however much ya like)
Hot pepper if ya like
Salt and pepper
1 lb. pasta or rice

Preheat oven to 350°F.

In a large casserole dish, place the chicken pieces along with the tomatoes, onions, olives, and peppers.

Add the olive oil and the water.

Stir, making sure the chicken pieces and vegetables are coated with the liquids.

Sprinkle with the spices—just a bit of each—and mix again.

Cover and bake for 1 hour. Uncover and bake for 30 more minutes.

Serve with cooked pasta or rice and get ready ta find ya husband!

"Now, cacciatore means 'hunter.' So if yer hunting fer a husband, make dis nice dish to put you in da mood. He won't be able to resist!"

Or maybe yer hunting fa a wife. In that case, give me a call, doll.

Salad Antipasto

Serves 4–6

"This is ta die for, if I do say so myself. Ya could live on this fa weeks and feel so happy. If ya brought this over to a party, it would be such a kindness 'cause ya know they never had nothin' like it before. And ya know, when yas are kind to someone else, it makes you feel good too. Raises those endorphin things they are always talking about in da sports pages and health magazines!"

Marinade:

⅔ cup extra virgin olive oil
½ cup red wine vinegar
2 cloves garlic, pressed
1 tsp basil
1 tsp. oregano
1 tsp. parsley
Red pepper flakes
Salt and pepper

Note: Youse can always add more of these spices. It depends on ya taste.

Mix marinade ingredients togetha in a large bowl and add:

1 medium (10-oz.) jar peperoncini peppers, drained
1 (14-oz.) can black olives, drained and halved
1 medium (14-oz.) jar stuffed green olives, drained and halved
1 large carrot, sliced
2 stalks celery, sliced
1 (8-oz.) can artichoke hearts (If packed in water, drain. If packed in oil, you can add it all.)
1 lb. fresh mushrooms parboiled in red wine vinegar and water
(Sometimes I joosta put them in fresh.)

Mix dis all up good!

Cover and put marinade mixture in refrigerator for 1 or 2 hours.

Or ya can leave it on da counter if the weather's not too hot. That's what we used ta do in da old days.

Salad:

1 head iceberg lettuce, chopped
½ lb. provolone, diced
½ lb. salami, diced
2 cucumbers, sliced
2 tomatoes, chopped

Mix togetha.

Put some salad on a plate, as much as youse want. Then put some of the nice marinade mixture on top.

The marinade will keep in the refrigerator. And youse can eat it anytime with crusty bread for a delicious snack.

Think I'll go make some right now.

"We're savin' big money here!"

Chickpeas and Egg Noodles

Serves 4–6

We never had a proper recipe fa this kind of cookin', but I know youse can figure it out. Dis shows ya that once yas learn about cooking, youse can cook "from ya head." Dat's what my mamma used ta say! We don't need no recipe!

Take ya ½-inch-wide egg noodles and cook 8 ounces, makin' sure to cook them al dente.

Drain.

Sauté up some fresh chopped garlic in olive oil.

To the sautéed garlic, add 1 large (28-oz.) can of crushed tomatoes or some fresh tomato puree ya made wid tomatoes from ya garden (or ya neighbor's garden).

Add some oregano and basil if ya like. Maybe some salt and pepper too. Add 1 can of chickpeas/cannellini beans, drained.

Mix it all together with the noodles.

Bring to almost boiling, and mangia!

"Now this is one of da old recipes we made when we didn't have much moola ... ya know wad I mean?! We knew it was good fa ya, though. So here we got good-fa-yas ... so easy ta make ... and so cheap too! Turns out that often the old ways are best. Besides, ya can give it to ya friends ya don't like so much and save money!"

"La dolce vita! I mean it!"

Pasta Carbonara

Serves 4–6

5 eggs
4 oz. heavy cream
Salt, joosta pinch
1 Tbsp. olive oil
2 Tbsp. butter
½ lb. bacon
1 lb. pasta, any kind yas like
1¼ cups mixed Romano and Parmesan cheese
Freshly cracked pepper

In a bowl, beat the eggs and cream together with da pinch of salt.

In a large skillet, heat oil and butter. Add the bacon and cook till crisp. Remove bacon and crumble.

Cook the pasta, al dente of course. Drain the pasta and add it to the skillet along with the crumbled bacon. Stir well.

Remove skillet from heat and stir in the beaten egg mixture with half of the cheese mixture.

Stir quickly to coat the pasta with the mixture. Then stir in the rest of the cheese.

Add some fresh pepper if ya like, and yer done.

This is so easy yas can make it fa unexpected company, and they'll think yer wonderful!

"So da kids move out and ya think ya don't have ta cook anymore. But let me tell ya, they always come home ta get a free meal! Ya make 'em this in no time, fills dem up, and ya don't have ta do much work! And ya know, they always bring their laundry home, so be ready."

"Don't ya love these
glasses, doll?"

Spaghetti
with Anchovies

Serves 4–6

2 (2-oz.) cans plain anchovies
3 Tbsp. olive oil
3 cloves garlic, minced
1 lb. thin spaghetti
Parmesan cheese

Put the anchovies and their liquid into a frying pan on low heat. Simmer until they break up. Use a wooden spoon to mix them up.

Then add the olive oil and turn the heat up to medium for about 1 minute.

Add the garlic, turn the heat to low, and simmer for another 5 minutes, being careful not to burn the garlic.

By now it smells so good ya might have ta dip a nice piece of Italian bread into da frying pan, joosta take a taste!

Take ya cooked spaghetti. Put in a nice bowl, and add anchovy sauce. Mix thoroughly and serve with grated Parmesan cheese.

This is something ya can make anytime.
So good, so quick, and gives ya lots of time
ta do other tings. Ooh fa!

"So maybe ya never made this kinda food before. Well, ya gotta take some risks, ya know? It spices up ya life and makes ya feel good. Besides, when ya try new things and learn new things, it keeps ya brain happy. And when yer happy and spicy, it's easy to find and give love."

"What's better than ta all
be together, sharing food
and love?"

Spaghetti Puttanesca

Serves 4–6

3 Tbsp. olive oil
3 cloves garlic, minced
1–2 (2-oz.) cans plain anchovy fillets
1 (14-oz.) can crushed or diced tomatoes
1 cup black olives, chopped
2 Tbsp. pine nuts or chopped wlanuts
¼ tsp. capers
1 lb. spaghetti
Parsley, for garnish
Parmesan cheese
Salt and pepper

Heat olive oil in frying pan. Add minced garlic and anchovy fillets with liquid. Cook gently until they begin to break up. Use wooden spoon to stir.

Now stir in tomatoes, black olives, nuts, and capers. Cook gently for 5 more minutes.

Serve over cooked spaghetti. Sprinkle with parsley, Parmesan cheese, and salt and pepper too, if ya like.

This is very good ta have on Christmas Eve even if ya gonna have the Seven Fish Feast!

Call me if ya don't know what dat means!

"With this one, ya get fancy. Sometimes when I eat this, I have good dreams. Ya know all da old ladies down at da market say that ya gotta listen ta ya dreams. Dreams can give ya good wisdom 'cause they come from that other place, wherever dat is!"

Red Clam Sauce for Linguini

Serves 4–6

2 Tbsp. olive oil
2 cloves garlic, finely chopped
1 onion, chopped
3 stalks celery, chopped
¼ tsp. thyme
¼ tsp. dried basil
½ tsp. oregano
Salt and pepper
2 cups canned chopped tomatoes
1 (6-oz.) can tomato paste
1½ cups water
2 cups bottled or fresh clam juice
2 cups minced clams, fresh or canned
¼ cup butter
¼ cup chopped parsley
1 lb. linguini
Parmesan cheese

Heat olive oil in a heavy skillet. Add garlic, onion, and celery. Stir together. Cook until the onion is soft.

Add thyme, basil, oregano, salt and pepper, tomatoes, tomato paste, and water. Bring to a boil, reduce heat, and simmer gently, uncovered, for 30 minutes.

Add the clam juice and cook for 25 minutes.

Add the clams and cook gently
for 5 more minutes.

Stir in the butter and parsley, and simmer
until the butter melts.

Serve over freshly cooked linguini
with Parmesan cheese.

Now if yas wanna
really make dis
a meal to remember,
go down ta the
seashore. There
yas can dig the
clams yaselves.
Well, have da kids
dig the clams
while yas sit
there and sip a
little red wine
ta get in da
mood for this
fabulous food!

"Hey, don't walk away
from me like that!
Don't ya got no
respect!"

35

"This one's fa love!"

Caponata

Serves 4–6

2 medium eggplants, peeled and diced
½ cup olive oil
2½ cups thinly sliced onions
1 cup thinly sliced celery
1 large (28-oz.) can tomato puree
¼ cup red wine vinegar
1 Tbsp. sugar
2 Tbsp. capers
½ tsp. salt
Dash of pepper
12 black olives, sliced

In a large frying pan, sauté the eggplant in the olive oil.

Remove the eggplant when soft, and sauté the onion and celery.

Return the eggplant to the pan, and add the tomato puree.

Bring to a boil, and then reduce heat and simmer 15 minutes.

Add the vinegar, sugar, capers, salt, pepper, and olives. Simmer, covered, for 20 minutes.

Refrigerate overnight.

Now truth is, ya can do it in da morning and serve it at night if ya forget ta make it da day before. It's gonna give ya lots of those antioxy things they talk about in the news, which keep ya healthy!

Youse can have it wid crackers or crusty sliced Italian bread.

Sometimes I don't use da sugar 'cause I am trying to stay slim, ya know!

"Eating dis makes ya heart sing. It is so good that I'm hungry joosta tinking about it! Ya know, music an' singing makes those endorphin tings jump up and down. And when dat happens, lookout! Ya gonna feel so good, ya can do anything!"

"Wid legs like dese a girl can go
anywhere she wants!"

Macaroni with Sausage and Zucchini

Serves 4–6

1 Tbsp. olive oil
5 Italian sausage links, hot or mild
1 clove garlic, chopped
1 large (28-oz.) can crushed tomatoes
1 tsp. dried oregano
1 Tbsp. parsley
Salt and pepper
3–4 small zucchinis, sliced
1 lb. macaroni, any kind ya like
Parmesan cheese

Add olive oil and sausage to a frying pan and brown well. Remove sausage from the pan.

Add garlic and cook gently for 2 minutes, stirring all the while, being careful not ta burn it.

Add the crushed tomatoes, oregano, parsley, salt, and pepper, and return sausage to pan.

Bring to a boil and then reduce to a simmer. Add zucchini to top of sauce and simmer, covered, for 45 minutes.

Serve mixed with cooked macaroni, sprinkled with Parmesan cheese.

Probably ya wanna use turkey sausage now so yas don't have too much fat. But I gotta tell ya, sometimes a little fat is a good thing.

"So ... it's late ... yas are all hungry. Wadda ya gonna make? Now's da time ta get creative. Ya always have dis stuff in da house ... or ya should. Ya throw it all togetha like I'm telling ya right here. And wadda ya got? Ya got a feast fit fer a King, dat ya made yaself. 'Cause ya got respect!!"

Veal Escalopes and Fettuccine Verde

Serves 4–6

"Once and a while, ya gotta go deluxe and make nice wid some big shots from da office. This meal is gonna knock their socks off. Shows ya creativity, shows ya got respect, shows yer a high-class person dat can deal wid everyone and anything."

1 clove garlic, crushed
2–3 Tbsp. olive oil
½ tsp. oregano
½ tsp. basil
1 cup sliced mushrooms
1½ lbs. veal cutlet or veal for stewing
½ cup marsala wine or sherry
½ cup beef stock
Salt and pepper
2 Tbsp. chopped parsley
1 lb. green fettuccini

Sauce:

2 oz. butter
1¼ cup heavy cream
2 oz. Parmesan cheese, grated (⅔ cup)
Salt and pepper

Add 1 clove crushed garlic to unheated oil in heavy skillet. Heat oil slowly, and add oregano, basil, and mushrooms.

Add veal and brown on each side.

Heat wine in a small saucepan and ignite. When the flames die down, add the wine to the skillet.

Stir in stock. Add salt and pepper to taste.

Cover and simmer for 12–15 minutes till veal is tender. Uncover and reduce liquid till gravy is smooth. Stir if needed.

To make the sauce, melt butter. Add cream and cheese plus salt and pepper to taste. Stir over medium heat until cheese has melted and sauce is thick.

Mix sauce and the chopped parsley with cooked fettuccini, making sure all strands of the pasta are coated. Then serve wid the veal and ya got ya meal.

"So I sez ta them, make more gravy!"

If ya want, yas can have salad first. Ya guests won't know what hit them!

Pasta Fagioli

Serves 4–6

Cannellini beans
(Ya need about 1½ cups. If they are from a can, just rinse them.
If they are dried, follow the soaking directions on the package.)

Water, maybe 3½ cups
1 (14-oz.) can of plum tomatoes, chopped and with da juice
3 cloves garlic, crushed
2 bay leaves
Salt and pepper
Some olive oil, maybe 2 or 3 Tbsp. and a little more fa the dipping sauce
2½ cups ditalini (if yas can't find ditalini, use any small pasta)
Fresh parsley, chopped—a nice handful
Parmesan cheese

Ya know, in some parts of this country ya can't even find fresh garlic, let alone ditalini! I even met someone who never chopped fresh garlic. Wadda ya gonna do?

Anyway, back to da recipe ...

So put da beans in a big pot. Cover wid water. Add the tomatoes, garlic, bay leaves, salt and pepper, and oil. (And by da way, ya can add a chopped carrot and onion if ya want.)

Bring to a boil, then reduce heat and simmer for about 2 hours. Now, ya can put some of this mixture through a sieve or a food processor if ya want and add it back to da pot. (We never do that, but some others did.)

"Well, we really say pasta fazhool. It's a whole meal and so healthy fa ya and so cheap to make. What more could ya want!? Joosta shows wad ya can do wid simple things like our nonnas told us."

"It would be so kind ta make dis fa ya sick friends. Nonna always said kindness comes back to ya, and since we all need lots of kindness ... do it."

As it simmers youse can add some more water if ya need to.

After 2 hours bring this all back to a boil and add the ditalini.
Cook till pasta is just done, maybe 10 minutes.

Garnish with parsley, and then ya serve it wid a dipping sauce of a bit of
olive oil and some Parmesan cheese. Ya gotta have lots of cheese. This
sauce is so good even wid just some crusty bread.

I'm hungry joosta
thinking about it!

"Think about
the little
nice things
everyday.
Put them in
ya 'joy pot'
und cook it
all up!"

Cheese Raviolis

Serves 4–6

Dough:
4 cups flour
2 eggs
1 Tbsp. olive oil
¾ tsp. salt
1 cup warm water to mix, of course use more if yas need it

Joosta in case ya don't know how ta do this dough, I will tell yas.

Put the flour in the middle of a nice clean board or smooth counter.

Make a well in the flour.

Crack the eggs into the well and add da olive oil, salt, and water.

Youse can use a fork or ya fingers ta beat those eggs wid da oil, salt, and water and slowly take flour from da sides of the well to combine wid the eggs mixture. Keep doing this until a big ball is formed.

Move ball to the side, flour the board and knead the dough gently until it is light and smooth. The dough should be nice and light. Don't knead it too much. If it starts to feel hard and heavy, then yas done it too long. Start again!

Filling:
3 lbs. ricotta cheese
3 eggs
Salt and pepper
Romano cheese—a big handful
2 Tbsp. chopped parsley

Parmesan cheese
1 recipe Gravy (see page 8)

Mix all filling ingredients well.

Roll out da dough into two sheets—not too thin, not too thick, maybe ⅛ inch.

> "These are a special treat and alotta work, but every minute is worth it 'cause while yer making, yer talking wid ya family and friends. It's like a big party. Well, it is a big party! Then yas sit down ta eat ... there's so much happiness ... along wid da nice red wine and lots of laughter. So mangia!"

"So what's not
ta like?"

Drop nice big tablespoons of filling along one sheet of da dough,
about 2 inches apart.

Cover wid the otha sheet of dough and press down softly.

Use one of dos zig zagged pastry wheels and cut da dough in
between da filling ta make nice ravioli shapes.

Leave to dry on floured cloth or board or … anyting ya got dat's flat.
They gotta dry fa at least 30 minutes before ya cook 'em.

Now if ya want to freeze 'em, just put them in a nice plastic bag
and pop them in da freezer.

When it is time ta cook them, bring a nice big pot of water to a boil and
gently put the raviolis in it.

Cook 'em until they float up to da top (for frozen, maybe 20 minutes,
for fresh, less).

Cover wid gravy ya made yaself from my recipe on
page 8. Eat and enjoy!

45

Zeppole

Serves 4–6

"Ya wanna talk about love? Making these on Christmas Eve fa ya family and friends is love, love, love. Every time ya knead da dough, it's like yer sending love out ta everyone ya know. All da family fries them together. So ya got happy times, traditions, singing, endorphins, joy ... I mean ya got da whole cannoli ... Amen ta that, I say."

1 package yeast (2¼ tsps.)
3–4 cups warm water
3½ lbs. flour
2 Tbsp. olive oil
2–3 Tbsp. salt
1 egg, beaten
Crisco
Vegetable oil

Powdered sugar

Dissolve yeast in 1 cup warm water.

Put the flour in a big pot, making a well. Add the olive oil, salt, and egg to the well.

Then add the yeast and water solution.

Mix the dough togetha, slowly adding enough warm water to make a nice, soft dough. This usually takes about 3 more cups.

Turn onto a floured board. Knead till smooth and elastic.

When ya kneading the dough, it's good. Ya using lots of muscles and that make ya strong. The wonderful smell and feel of da dough make ya feel so happy. It is almost like saying ya prayers!

Grease a big pot with Crisco, and then sprinkle the pot with a little more flour. Put da dough in da pot, and grease da top of da dough with Crisco too.

Put a damp cloth over the pot and set in a warm place to rise (like on a chair by ya stove).

Then whoever is in the kitchen with ya should join hands and say a Hail Mary over da pot of dough. If ya don't know that prayer, call me. I'll teach ya!

Let the dough rise till doubled in bulk.

Ya feel so happy 'cause now it is almost ready!

So now ya punch da dough down. Flour ya surface—like ya dough board or ya counter if ya got no big board. Take a nice sharp knife and cut off dough pieces da size of a baby's fist. Stretch each one out and make an oval, pressing with your thumbs to make a hole in da middle. Ya can twist it if ya want and make a figure eight shape.

Set these on da floured surface ta rise again fa about 10 minutes. I cover 'em wid a cloth so they don't dry out.

Meanwhile in a big pot, put enough vegetable oil to fill da pot halfway. Heat it up till it is so hot that when ya put a little piece of dough in, it floats right to da top.

Now be careful here 'cause oil can burn ya if ya not careful. Don't let da kids near da pot. I use long tongs ta put da dough in and take it out.

So when it is hot enough, then ya take the ovals and ya gently put 'em in da oil. Fry on one side till golden, turn over, and do the other side.

When they are done, ya put them on a plate which is covered wid a paper towel.

If ya like, ya can sprinkle wid powdered sugar.

When they are cool, ya can cover wid foil or put them in a brown paper bag to keep them from getting too hard. When they get hard, ya can dunk 'em in hot chocolate or sweet coffee. When they are very hard, den they are great fa ya little ones who are teething.

"Say a Hail Mary over da pot — if ya don't know that prayer, call me. I'll teach ya! It works fa everybody, no matter what."

"Gimme a big slice, doll!"

Lena's Cheesecake

Serves 8–10

3 lbs. cream cheese, softened
8 eggs
1¾ cups very fine sugar
2 tsp. vanilla essence
2 oz. half and half

Preheat the oven to 350°F.

Cream half the cheese with 4 eggs. Beat until smooth. Then add the rest of the cheese and the remaining 4 eggs. Beat until smooth.

Add sugar, vanilla, and half and half.

Continue beating till creamy and smooth.

(This step takes a long time, so don't rush it, doll!)

Pour into a greased 9-inch springform pan.

Bake for 1 hour and do not open the oven door!

Then turn off the oven, open the oven door slightly, and let the cake cool in the oven for 1 more hour.

Take it out and cool for another hour, and then refrigerate. Serve chilled.

This is ta die for! I like it joosta plain wid nothing on top tu spoil da taste.

"Madonna mia, wad am I gonna tell ya about this? This is pure joy, and yas know we are all meant fa joy. Ya just gotta accept da joy ... so take a bite and say yes ta joy."

49

Fashion Tips from Aunt Lena

If ya wanna cook right,
yas gotta look right!

Turn the page
fa some ideas...

A selection from
'LENA'S LINE: clothes fa the woman
who knows what she wants.

About the Author

Born in New York City, raised in Northern New Jersey, Anne-Louise Sterry is the eldest daughter of a large Italian family where music and storytelling have always been a big part of her life. Family get–togethers and holidays were celebrated with music and stories, not just food. At summer family gatherings at the Jersey shore, she and her siblings would fall asleep to the sounds of aunts and uncles singing and laughing at old stories. It was those early family experiences that inspired Anne-Louise to take the first steps toward becoming a professional singer and storyteller. In the years since she has performed across the United States, in Europe, and added keynote speaking and staff development programs to her work.

Anne-Louise's repertoire is extensive and encompasses many genres from the sublime to the hilarious. Her most endearing creation is Aunt Lena, Anne-Louise's alter ego in the guise of everyone's crazy Italian relative. Aunt Lena mixes stories from the New Jersey homeland with cutting–edge Mediterranean wisdom such as choosing joy, the importance of home–cooked food, and the gift of love and family. When Aunt Lena speaks, there's no telling what might happen.